I0171957

Reigniting

Your

Marriage

How to bring back love and

intimacy into your relationship.

By

Toyin Fakorede

Copyright © 2015

By Toyin Fakorede

Published by:

WINNING FAITH
OUTREACH MINISTRIES

London . New York . Lagos

ISBN: 978-1-907095-14-6

All scriptures are taken from New King James Version (NKJV) unless otherwise stated.

Content

Reigniting your marriage

Dedication

This book is dedicated to my adorable wife,

my one and only

Gbemisola Esther Fakorede.

Reigniting your marriage

Acknowledgements

First, I wish to thank my mentor Dr. Charles Omole who has really helped to stir my life and ministry in the right direction in God. Thank you for your continued support and wise counsel.

I would also like to thank Dayo Elugbaju and Joy Johnson, my ardent and dedicated editors. Thank you for being thorough and ensuring that the content meets the required standard.

My gratitude goes to my darling wife Gbemisola and our beautiful daughter Bunmi, for your understanding and continual support in allowing me to do all that God has put in my heart to accomplish. I love you both dearly.

Reigniting your marriage

Foreword

There is something about the institution of marriage that perhaps gives most people a sense that they know more about it than they really do. After all, which other institution gives you a certificate at the start of your engagement with it rather than at the end. Marriage is a complex institutions that requires the input and steadfast companionship of Christ to make a success of it.

With the war against marriages by secular humanism and liberal mentality that is taking over the world; it is time we provide valuable tools to equip couples and strengthen relationships. Nobody is born with all the knowledge; we must work to acquire it. This is why I am happy with this major contribution to the marriage and relationship library by Pastor Toyin. This book excels by its simplicity but still deep and profound information that is bound to strengthen your marriage and relationships. It combines spiritual principles with practical applications in a way that works perfectly.

This book is an essential addition to your library if you care about reigniting the passion you once had or maintain the fire of love and romance in your marriage. It is instructive but easy to read. I recommend this book to all who seek to make their marriages the best it can be. An essential lesson in marriage is that you are always learning, always improving. This book will give you the vital tools and tips needed to make your marriage like heaven on the earth.

Time spent reading this book is a valuable investment into your marriage and you will see an almost immediate return as your paradigm is adjusted scripturally to begin to fully enjoy your marriage as God intended. This could be the best book you will read and enjoy for a long time to come. I congratulate you on a wise decision that is guaranteed to make you a better lover and an exciting partner for your spouse. It is going to be awesome.

Dr Charles Omole
President / Serving Overseer
Winning Faith Outreach Ministries Intl.

Reigniting your marriage

Reigniting your marriage

Introduction

Revelation 2:4-5 *"Nevertheless I have this against you, that you have left your first love. Remember therefore from where you have fallen; repent and do the first works, or else I will come to you quickly and remove your lampstand from its place unless you repent"*

The relationship between the husband and his wife is symbolic of the relationship between Christ and the church. Paul described this special union to the church in Ephesus in Ephesians 5:23-25*"For the husband is head of the wife, as also Christ is the head of the church; and He is the Saviour of the body. Therefore, just as the* *church is subject to Christ, so let the wives be to their own husbands in everything. Husbands love your wives, just as Christ also loved the church and gave Himself for her. "*

Christ has demonstrated His unconditional, unfailing and boundless love to His church. This sets a standard for the husband; to be a loving and nurturing husband.

Ephesians 5:33 *"Nevertheless let each one of you in particular so love his own wife as himself and let the wife see that she respects her husband."*

It is important to note that an unregenerate mind cannot express love because it is evil, we cannot give what we don't have: Jeremiah 17:9 *"The heart is deceitful above all things, and desperately wicked; who can know it?"* A heart that is not surrendered to Jesus cannot love like Jesus. That is why the new birth is required, the moment we become born again, we become a new creature and we receive a new heart. Our heart gets circumcised by the Holy Spirit and the love of God is poured into our hearts.

Romans 5:5 "......*the love of God has been poured out in our hearts by the Holy Spirit who was given to us*".

Likewise, the wife has been commanded to submit to the leadership of the husband in the home just as the church is subject to Christ being the head of the church.

The church being subject to Christ is not an act of subjugation but an act of worship and reference to Christ in a loving and rewarding manner. In like manner, the wife submits to the authority of her husband not because she has been vanquished by him but she willingly and lovingly surrenders herself to his headship.

This is depicted by the wife changing her father's name to start bearing the name of her beloved husband.

The Church in Ephesus received a direct message from the Lord through John the beloved that they had forsaken their first love. Even though, the Lord commended their works, labour, patience, perseverance but their flame of love had been quenched.

Similarly, several husbands can be commended for their diligence, business intelligence, keeping up with the bills, providing for the family but have lost the spark in the relationship with their wives and vice versa. There are certain indicators that reveal that a relationship has lost its spark such as when argument becomes the order of the day, when love making becomes a chore rather than a pleasure, when both parties rarely compliment or appreciate each other, when communication is only limited to responsibilities they have to fulfil.

As a result of this loss, many couples have forgone their relevance in the home. *"Remember therefore from where you have fallen; repent and do the first works, or else*

I will come to you quickly and remove your lampstand from its place – unless you repent"

The purpose of this book is to help restore your love life, re-establish intimacy and romance in your marriage, understand the needs of your spouse, stay spiritually connected to your spouse, resolve conflicts and stay strong in your relationship.

Reigniting your marriage

CHAPTER I

Understand the Needs of your Spouse

Matthew 19:8 *"He said to them, "Moses, because of the hardness of your hearts, permitted you to divorce your wives, but from the beginning it was not so."*

Divorce is not God's idea but people get divorced because of the state of their heart. It was part of the consequences of the fall of mankind in that the heart of man became corrupted, wicked and insensitive.

Matthew 15:19*"For out of the heart proceed evil thoughts, murders, adulteries,* *fornications, thefts, false witness, blasphemies."*

We are products of the thoughts in our hearts. If the heart is not fixed, mankind cannot be fixed. Religion cannot fix the heart, only God can fix the heart and He did that at Calvary.

We receive a renewed heart when we surrender our lives to Jesus Christ. We are told in Romans 5:5 that the love of God has been poured out in our hearts by the Holy Spirit who has been given to us. This implies that it is difficult for an un-renewed heart to show perfect love. You can only give what you have.

Only a heart that is filled with the love of God can give unconditional love. The Greek language calls this kind of love Agape which means good will, benevolence, divine love. Agape is not dependent on how you feel about what your spouse has done or refused to do. Agape comes from God and enables you to love your spouse regardless.

Ephesians 5:25 *"Husbands, love your wives, just as Christ also loved the church and gave Himself for her."*

He loved the church unconditionally and sacrificially. The scripture has instructed the husband to love the wife unconditionally and sacrificially. The wife should likewise love the husband unconditionally as what is good for the goose is good for the gander.

Without such love, you cannot put the needs of your spouse ahead of yours.

Parasitic and Symbiotic Relationship

In elementary biology, we were taught two basic types of relationships between living organisms: Parasitic and Symbiotic relationship. A parasitic relationship is one in which one an organism (the parasite) lives off of another organism (the host), thereby causing harm to the host e.g ticks, lice and leeches.

On the other hand, a symbiotic relationship is an interaction with mutual benefit to both organisms. For example: A bullhorn Acacia tree provides food and shelter for the ant and in return, the ant offers protection by attacking organisms such as grasshoppers, caterpillars and other tree species that pose a threat to the tree. The word symbiosis means living together. For these organisms to benefit from their association there must be mutual understanding of their needs.

Similarly, if we want our relationships to be beneficial, we must first of all understand the needs of our partner. Amos 3:3 *"Can two walk together unless they are agreed."*

The needs of married couples are so compelling that when they are unsatisfied in marriage, there is so much hurt and frustration that the temptation to go outside of marriage to satisfy such needs becomes more potent. On the other hand, when needs are satisfied, there is marital bliss and the marriage is protected against infidelity and separation.

Separation and Divorce statistics

I want to share some relevant UK facts and figures. According to separation and divorce statistics filed by Relate [1] (UK's largest provider of relationship support) in 2014; the report stated that *"relationships come under immense pressure from demands of children and family, work, home and money difficulties. Furthermore, as people change and grow through life, their needs and desires can be expected to diversify. Marriages and long-term relationships do not always survive the strain."* [2]

The report also revealed that 42% of marriages end in divorce in England & Wales, the average age of people divorcing is between 42 and 45 years and 65% of divorces were on petition of the wife.
Reasons for divorce based on the report:
-   14% were granted for adultery

---

[1] http://www.relate.org.uk/files/relate/separation-divorce-factsheet-jan2014.pdf
[2] http://www.relate.org.uk/files/relate/separation-divorce-factsheet-jan2014.pdf

- 37% of divorces granted to men and 54% of divorces granted to women were due to unreasonable behaviour. (I believe this includes insensitivity to one another's needs)
- 32% of divorces granted to men and 22% of divorces granted to women were granted following 2 years of separation and consent
- 17% of divorces granted to men and 9% of divorces granted to women were granted following 5 years of separation

The above figures indicate that lack of understanding of the needs of your spouse leads to divorce even more than adultery. In fact, the most common reason for infidelity or adultery is unsatisfied emotional need.

Scriptural basis for understanding your spouse

Someone may argue that if I put the needs of my spouse before mine, what if he/she ignores my needs, what do I do? Remember that the goal of this book is to bring back love and intimacy into your relationship. Therefore, someone would need to pay the price to re-ignite the spark and that person is you.

For God so loved the world that He gave His only Son (John 3:16). What a sacrifice! Today, many of us are in relationship with God because of the sacrifice He made. In like manner, you must be prepared to make sacrifices to restore the love you once shared with your spouse.

Let us examine 3 key words from the first epistle of Peter to couples and other fellow believers in I Peter 3:1-9.

"*1. Wives, likewise, be submissive to your own husbands, that even if some do not obey the word, they without a word, may be won by the **conduct** of their wives.*

2. When they observe your chaste conduct accompanied by fear.

3. Do not let your adornment be merely outward-arranging the hair, wearing gold, or putting on fine apparel-

[4.] *rather let it be the* **hidden person of the heart**, *with the incorruptible beauty of a* <u>*gentle and quiet spirit*</u>, *which is very precious in the sight of God.*

[5.] *For in this manner, in former times, the holy women who trusted in God also adorned themselves, being submissive to their own husbands,*

[6.] *as Sarah obeys Abraham, calling him lord, whose daughters you are if you do good and are not afraid with any terror.*

[7.] *Husbands, likewise, dwell with them with* **understanding**, *giving* <u>*honor*</u> *to the wife as to the weaker vessel and as being heirs together of the grace of life, that your prayers may not be hindered.*

[8.] *Finally, all of you be of* <u>*one mind*</u>, *having* <u>*compassion*</u> *for one another, love as brothers, be* <u>*tenderhearted*</u>, *be* <u>*courteous*</u>;

[9.] <u>*not returning evil for evil*</u> *or reviling for reviling, but on the contrary blessing, knowing that you were called to this, that you may inherit a blessing."*

I have underlined some key words in the above scripture; I will discuss only 3 and leave the rest until chapter six. The first key word is **Conduct.** When your spouse observes your chaste or unblemished conduct they may be won. The manner you conduct yourself in the home is capable of winning over your spouse or repelling them. Your conduct should be worthy of emulation.

It is counterproductive to try to meet the needs of your spouse while your conduct is repulsive. If you desire a positive response from your spouse, then be positive in your conduct. Let the change begin with you; become the change you desire in your relationship. Jesus said *"do unto others what you want them do to you* (Matthew 7:12)". Like begets like. Your conduct is determined by the values you uphold. Peter said your conduct should be accompanied by fear (respect).

I heard the story of a Pastor whose wife was always disrespectful and mean to him but he never treated her in the manner she deserved, rather he went to God in prayers, committing his marriage into God's hands and never ceased to express his love towards her.

One night the Lord visited his wife in a vision and He showed her a coffin. Then the Lord said to her if she would care to open the coffin to see who was inside. When she opened the coffin, she found herself inside. Then the Lord said, if she continues to ill-treat her husband, she would end up in that coffin.

When she woke up, she was scared to death. She repented and her attitude changed towards her husband. They have enjoyed marital bliss since then.

The second key word is the **Hidden Person of the Heart**. The hidden person of the heart is your spirit. Peter is saying as much as you spend time and resources on your outward appearance; clothes, shoes, jewelleries, you should spend time and resources in beautifying and growing your spirit. Why? Most conflicts in relationships are traceable to the manifestation of the works of the flesh – anger, hatred, pride, adultery, self-centeredness etc.

James 4:1 "*Where do those fights and quarrels among you come from? They come from your selfish desires that are at war in your bodies, don't they.*" (International Standard Version).

When we grow our spirit, we act less in the flesh.

Galatians 5:16 "*I say then: Walk in the Spirit, and you shall not fulfil the lust of the flesh.*"

You can't walk in the Spirit and be wrong. Grow where it matters, become mature in the Spirit and see how your actions, responses and decisions are influenced by the Holy Spirit.

The third key word is **Understanding**. To understand your spouse means making an effort to study your partner in order to understand their mannerism, moods, likes and dislikes etc.

Someone once said to me during a counselling session: "Is my wife so complex that I need a manual to operate her?" Human beings are complex in nature; what do you expect when two unique persons from different backgrounds, mindsets, intelligences, temperaments, desires, aspirations, likes and dislikes decide to live together? When two or more organisations want to partner, they sign a document called Memorandum of Understanding (MOU). This is a legal document outlining the terms and details of any agreement between parties, including each party's requirements and responsibilities. The day you married your spouse, you signed an MOU, even though the responsibilities and requirements are unwritten, each person has expectations to be satisfied by the other party. It therefore becomes necessary to study your spouse to understand her needs or expectations.

If someone falls sick, the sickness is diagnosed by examining the symptoms. However, if the doctor keeps treating the symptoms without dealing with the virus or the cause of the sickness, the symptoms would keep relapsing until the source is dealt with. In a similar fashion, most problems we face in marriage are symptoms of the main issue – unsatisfied needs/expectations.

Reigniting your marriage

CHAPTER TWO

What your Spouse Needs from You

Before we discuss what your spouse needs from you, I would like you and your partner to engage in an exercise. The purpose of the exercise is to reveal the extent to which your partner understands your expectations. I have outlined 10 basic marital needs below:

10 Basic Marital Needs
1. Friendship/Affection
2. Communication
3. Domestic Support
4. Financial Support
5. Spiritual Growth

6. Physical Attractiveness
7. Appreciation
8. Marital Security
9. Hubby buddy
10. Sexual Fulfilment

Take a piece of paper and write down 5 needs of your partner in order of priority. Your partner should do the same. The exercise should be done independently. Please do not allow your partner to see your note until you both have finished.

Now reveal your answers and compare them.

Has your partner been able to identify your needs? Are those needs in the right order? Now exchange your notes and make corrections accordingly.

Lastly, collect the corrected note and make a commitment to ensure you meet those needs. One of the reasons why couples find it difficult to satisfy the needs of their spouse is because the needs of the man is not usually the needs of the woman and the order of priority usually differs as demonstrated in the exercise earlier.

10 Things your spouse needs from you

1) Friendship/Affection

Affection is the cement of any relationship. Many couples were best of friends before they got married but after the wedding, the activities that catch the fancies of both parties begin to varnish due to several other life demands.

Therefore, affection in marriage is a virtue you must decide to consciously express to your spouse. It is important to note that a man's view of affection may be different from a woman's view and that is because of our different configurations.

To a woman hugs, gifts, flowers, holding of hands, kisses, romantic cards, romantic text messages are ways they perceive and receive affection but for some men, the only time they show affection is when they want to make love. If you keep working and fail to make time for your wife, she starts feeling neglected and resentful. Endeavour to find out how your spouse receives affection and express such to them.

2) Communication

What blood is to the body so is communication to any relationship. A group of students represented their institution at Microsoft Imagine Cup a few years ago.

The team made it up to the final stage, at the eve of the final competition, a member of the team made some changes to their software artefact without informing the other team members.

On the final day of the competition, the software failed to work leading to their defeat. Effective communication is what makes effective teamwork. Quality communication must be rich, honest, open, friendly and timely. Through communication other emotional needs are satisfied such as appreciation, show of affection, financial and domestic support.

Communication is necessary to discuss and solve everyday problem and to resolve conflict. Without communication, there isn't intimacy. Intimacy is not sex, rather it is the communication of how much you love and care for one another.

Intimacy is what breeds companionship. Communication is the key to bringing intimacy back into your marriage.

3) Domestic Support

Some women complain that their husbands don't help in house chores and that they create mess as much as the children do. You can become a blessing to your wife if you will clean up after yourself and inspire the children to do the same.

We have a policy in my house – everybody washes their plates. Remember your wife is neither your maid nor your mother. She is your partner. So the cleaning of the home is the responsibility of you both.

Many women have kindly assumed the responsibility of tidying up the home; it is only courteous to render support and to ensure that she is not worn out.

4) Financial Support

I once asked my audience during a teaching session, if women marry men for their money. I got varying answers but a lady gave a unique answer; she said, "*even if there is no physical money, there should be that potential*". Every woman would like a man who is capable of supporting himself and his family even if he is not very rich.

I Timothy 5:8"*But if anyone does not provide for his own and especially for those of his household, he has denied the faith and is worse than an unbeliever.*"

The man has the responsibility to provide for the family but sometimes it is difficult for one hand to provide for the whole family. The woman was created to be a help mate for the man.

Proverbs 31 describes a virtuous woman vs 15a "*She also rises while it is yet night, and provides food for her household......*" vs 28 "*Her children rise up and call her blessed; her husband also and he praises her.*"

It is important for every couple to discuss their finances, income and expenditure.

5) Spiritual Growth

God has placed the man in the position of a spiritual leader in the home. If God would speak to the family, He would speak to the man (that does not mean the woman cannot hear God for the family).

He spoke to Adam, and Adam passed the information to Eve. He is the God of Abraham, Isaac and Jacob and not the God of Sarah, Rebecca and Rachel. Therefore the woman needs a man that would inspire her faith in

God and challenge her to grow spiritually. In Ephesians 5:22-33, Paul juxtaposed the relationship between Christ and the church with the relationship between the husband and his wife. If Christ is the shepherd of the sheep, then it implies that the husband plays the role of a shepherd in the home.

Shepherds must provide the following:

i. Leadership: Become a role model for the children. Just as it is difficult for a bird to fly with one wing and it is difficult to clap with one hand, it is difficult (not impossible) for a single mother to raise her children. Every child needs a father figure. Submission to the man's authority in the home enables him to become a better leader.

ii. Sacrifice: John 10:11 *"I am the good shepherd. The good shepherd gives His life for the sheep."* Leadership comes with sacrifice. Sometimes you have to let go of your ego and rights to do the right thing for the general good of the marriage.

iii. Nourish and cherish: Ephesians 5:29 *"For no one ever hated his own flesh but nourishes and cherishes it, just as the Lord does the church."*

The Greek word for Nourish is Ektrepho which means to support her growth towards her own maturity. The Greek word for Cherish is Thalpo which means to warmly care for and attend to.

6) Physical Attractiveness

Sarah the wife of Abraham was a woman with a beautiful countenance (Genesis 12:11), Rebekah the wife of Isaac was very beautiful to behold (Genesis 24:16), Rachel the wife of Jacob was beautiful of form and appearance (Genesis 29:17). To most men and women physical attractiveness is a requirement. John once told his wife that he doesn't find her attractive anymore because she has increased in size.

Some people may argue that if John truly loves his wife he should love her the way she is. This is where we get it wrong. John has not stopped loving his wife, however he doesn't feel turned ON sexually by the physical appearance of his wife.

We all have sexual preferences and physical attractiveness has everything to do with love making. Weight loss, proper amount of exercise, right clothes, personal hygiene, make up, hairstyles are some ways to stay fit and maintain physical attractiveness.

7) **Appreciation**

The need for admiration, appreciation and respect is a requirement to be satisfied in every relationship. Every man wants to feel like a hero, he needs a woman to be proud of him. Every form of admiration a wife gives to her husband inspires him to do more and helps him to believe in himself. He wants to hear from his wife that he is smart, diligent, loving and good-looking.

Acknowledge his kind gestures; when he helps out in the kitchen, takes you out on a date or when he makes love to you. Appreciation serves as a reward for achievement.

As a man, make it a top priority to appreciate your wife; acknowledge the effort put towards every meal she prepares, admire her dressing, make-up, and hairstyle. Whatever we appreciate increases in value.

Many women feel frustrated in the home because their husbands complain more than they give compliments. If your wife is always on the defensive side, it may be that she is often being criticised. You know in your heart that your spouse is kind, honest and generous but you find it difficult to verbally express these qualities. Withholding such appreciation is wrong and repentance is needed.

God inhabits the praises of His people (Psalm 22:3). Praise invites His presence but complaints invoke His wrath (1 Corinthians 10:10). Similarly, everybody likes to stay in an atmosphere where they are cherished and desired. Make your company inviting by appreciating your spouse. It is a sure way to bring love and intimacy back into your relationship.

8) Marital Security

Trust is a vital requirement for a lasting relationship. A broken trust could take a while to rebuild in some cases it could take years. Therefore you want to ensure you don't betray the trust in your relationship. Your wife wants to be certain that you will not cheat on her and/or that she will not become secondary in your life.

Therefore she needs constant assurance of your love, devotion and loyalty. One of the elements that breed trust in relationships is transparency.

Genesis 2:25 *"And they were both naked, the man and his wife and were not ashamed."*

The two shall become one flesh – nothing hidden, nothing mysterious.

But someone may ask – what about my privacy?

Does my wife have the right to access my text messages, emails, social media accounts? In a healthy relationship, that should not be an issue because there is nothing to hide. Protecting your privacy makes you less transparent to your partner. What if my partner is not fond of my friends of the opposite sex?

I believe your spouse should feel comfortable with your friends of the opposite sex. If they feel uncomfortable with a particular friend, discuss any issues they might be having with your friendship and if they are still not comfortable because it is seen as a threat to your relationship, I think the best thing to do in this situation is to give up that friendship to protect your relationship. In my experience, the source of some of the problems couples face is lack of honesty.

The couple who upholds honesty and openness to each other especially about the source of anger or annoyance can identify such problems very quickly, discuss them and dispose them swiftly. I believe the more facts we have, the better we will understand one another. On the other hand, dishonesty or covering the truth is painfully offensive.

9) Hobby Buddy

People have hobbies like watching movies, playing computer games, football, cooking, reading, listening to music, dancing etc. Sometimes a woman gets annoyed that her husband is engaged in his hobby and this could create further problems because the man feels he is being denied of a legitimate need.

He may rather prefer to do it in his wife's absence or do it with friends. Therefore, your husband's hobby is an opportunity to get closer to him. Of course, I am not talking about activities that are detrimental to your morals or finances like gambling. Obviously, we must find mutual relaxation interests and this is done by communicating.

Decide to be interested in your partner's hobby, become your partner's hobby buddy.

10) Sexual Fulfilment

Without a doubt, men have higher degree of sexual drive than women. Many men have found themselves in situations where they literally beg their wives for sex. If sex is not a top priority for you as a woman, you should not in any way undermine your husband's desire to make love with you. He has restricted his sexual experience to his wife by covenant and he expects her to be as sexually interested in him as he is in her. Unmet sexual fulfilment could lead to frustration; while some will endure, others will find alternatives.

Sometimes, you may feel tired and unable to meet the sexual request of your spouse. Don't just dismiss his feeling, make him understand that you care about how he feels and promise him that you will make it up to him soonest.

Remember you may have a quickie (a brief act of sexual intercourse) if you feel tired or in a hurry to leave home. It is also good to set aside some time to have a banquet – 3 course meal of sexual activity. The sexual fulfilment of your spouse is your responsibility.

CHAPTER 3

Oneness in Marriage

Genesis 2:18-24 "*18. And the Lord God said, "It is not good that man should be alone; I will make him a helper comparable to him".* *19. Out of the ground the Lord God formed every beast of the field and every bird of the air, and brought them to Adam to see what he would call them. And whatever Adam called each living creature that was its name. 20. So Adam gave names to all cattle, to the birds of the air, and to every beast of the field. But for Adam there was not found a helper comparable to him. 21. And the Lord God caused a deep sleep to fall on Adam, and he slept; and He took one of his ribs and closed up the flesh in its place. 22. Then the rib which the Lord God had taken from man He made into a woman and He brought her to the man.* [23.] *And Adam said: "This is now the bone of my bones and flesh of my flesh; she shall be called Woman, because she was taken out of Man."* [24.] *Therefore a man shall leave his father and mother and be joined to his wife and they shall become one flesh."*

Adam was given a work to do – to tend the garden. Part of his job description was to name all animals and birds. Adam realised that he needed a helper in verse 20, but God already anticipated his need in verse 18 – *"it is not good for man to be alone......"*

Not until man realised that he needed a woman to assist him in carrying out his divine assignment, God did not give him a woman because he may not realise the purpose of the woman. Certain blessings will not come until we prove our readiness. When need is not established, value is not recognised. People tend to value whatever meets a need in their lives. Men who consider women to be additional responsibility for them do not seem to respect their wives as they ought to. Similarly, when a woman makes herself a liability to her husband without adding value to him or to the relationship, she tends to depreciate in value.

God calls the woman a helpmate or a partner. As a woman, it is important to know and understand the vision/purpose of your husband. Your destiny is not isolated from your husband's. Your husband's assignment is considered to be yours because you have been ordained by God to help him.

When God gave Adam the assignment and the commandment, He didn't need to communicate to Eve separately because Eve was in Adam in form of a rib (seed), so by extension both the assignment and the commandment applied to her. When she disobeyed the commandment (forbidden fruit), God did not say "you are exempted because it wasn't you I gave the commandment to." She faced the consequences of her actions.

If God gave Eve to Adam to assist him in carrying out his divine assignment, it implies that God has a divine purpose for every marriage. After all, every project should have aims and objectives, every research should have a research question. Every marriage is therefore, designed to fulfil a mandate. May God reveal to you the purpose of your marriage and enable you and your spouse to fulfil the same.

Teamwork is the ability to work together towards a common vision. To be successful, a team must have the following characteristics:

      I. Common goal
      II. Effective communication
      III. Sense of identity
      IV. Common values

Ecclesiastes 4:9-12 "[9] *Two are better than one, because they have a good reward for their labour. [10] For if they fall, one will lift up his companion. But woe to him who is alone when he falls, for he has no one to help him up. [11.] Again, if two lie down together, they will keep warm; but how can one be warm alone. [12.] Though one may be overpowered by another, two can withstand him. And a threefold cord is not quickly broken."*

Verse 9 speaks of synergy, verse 10 speaks of preservation, protection and restoration, verse 11 speaks of building up or developing together and verse 12 speaks of strength. A threefold cord speaks of you, your spouse and God. A relationship that involves God is difficult to break apart.

The ability to work cooperatively with others is one of the most valuable skills you can develop to accomplish your goals in career, business or pursuit.

A 20 years study was carried out at Stanford University. The study entailed careful observation of the career path of several executives to identify the qualities/skills they had either had or developed that enabled them to progress quickly. It was concluded that one of the qualities was team working.

A football team is trained to work cooperatively to achieve one goal – to win a match. Can you imagine if the players are not passing the ball to one another due to a disagreement they had before the match? I will leave the outcome of the match to your imagination.

You and your spouse are a team appointed by God to fulfil a divine assignment. Any marital conflict should be seen as a form of distraction from your common goal, therefore should be resolved as quickly as possible. We shall now discuss three couples in the bible.

Ahasuerus and Vashti Esther 1:1-12
King Ahasuerus was a very influential king who reigned over 127 provinces from India to Ethiopia. He ruled over Persia and Media. Verse 3 *"that in the third year of his reign*

he made a feast for all his officials and servants – the powers of Persia and Media, the nobles and the princes of the provinces being before him" verse 9 *"Queen Vashti also made a feast for the women in the royal palace which belonged to King Ahasuerus."*

My question is; why didn't Queen Vashti join her husband in the feast, why must she do hers separately? There are two possibilities; it could have been done in good fate to have a separate feast for the women, after all churches do have women group and the motive is not to separate them from their husbands or cause division but for edification and to share common concerns. It could also be that she wanted to host her feast separately to spite her husband or to show lack of interest in her husband's affairs.

Do you and your spouse do things separately or together? Some men don't allow their wives to be involved in their decision making process. Such men believe they are smart, as far as they are concerned their wives have no input in the conception and execution of their plans. If she tries to share her ideas, she gets shut down.

If you are that kind of man, you are pushing your wife away and depriving yourself of the help she is ordained to offer you. There is wisdom God has placed in your wife for you, two are better than one the scripture tells us. The virtue you don't value cannot flow towards you. You must learn to value and receive the blessing of the virtuous wife God has given to you.

Remember you were once friends and what brings friends together is the need for one another. A friend in need is a friend indeed they say. The key to intimacy is doing things together; watch movies together, cook together, plan together, pray together, play together, eat together etc.

In verse 10 -11"[10.] *On the seventh day when the heart of the King was merry with wine, he commanded Mehuman, Biztha, Harbona, Bigtha, Abagtha, Zethar and Carcas, seven eunuchs who served in the presence of King*

Ahasuerus, [11.] to bring Queen Vashti before the king, wearing her royal crown, in order to show her beauty to the people and the officials, for she was beautiful to behold. [12.] But Queen Vashti refused to come at the king's command brought by his eunuchs; therefore the king was furious and his anger burned within him."

There are certain points to note in these verses:

1. The Kings heart was merry with wine, International Standard Version of the bible says he was under the influence of the wine – he was not in his right mind and he commanded his wife to be brought in order to show her beauty to the people and the officials. We act irrationally when under some kind of negative influence. For some it could be alcohol, some men even physically abuse their wives when drunk. To another, it could be the influence of friends and even families (3rd parties in our relationship). Allowing other people to have a say

in your relationship prevents you and your spouse from cleaving properly. To another, it could be work pressure. People have different ways of responding to stress. Most people don't function optimally when under stress and if stress is not properly managed it could cause unnecessary arguments in our relationships. That is why it is necessary to make time for relaxation. It is important we learn how to eliminate these negative influences and be fully united with our spouses.

2. The Queen refused to come at the King's command because she was clearly not comfortable with the instruction. She dishonoured her husband and she lost her place. What she refused to do, several women were willing to compete to win the heart of her husband, and eventually Esther won. If there was love and understanding in their relationship, she should have gone to her husband and politely reasoned with him to

rethink his demands and to demonstrate her humility and honour. However, I suspect the reason she didn't bother to reason with her husband could be that Ahasuerus was one of those men who would not listen to their wives; they make themselves unapproachable, unsupportive and unfriendly. The atmosphere in your home should be such that supports openness and liberty to express oneself without the fear of judgement and condemnation.

3. Another notable point is that, the bible didn't say anything about her being remorseful and apologise to her husband or maybe she didn't even have the opportunity – she lost her home instantly. Apology could save us from unnecessary battles in our relationships. On the other hand the husband allowed other people to pronounce judgement on his own wife. The inclusion of third parties in your home will eventually wreck your

marriage. He could have forgiven his wife, because his anger eventually subsided and he remembered what had been decreed against her (Esther 2:1) but it was too late. In the heat of anger and pain, we sometimes involve third parties but we fail to realise is that we have rubbished our partner in the sight of external parties. Even when you both get reconciled, these parties already have an ill perception about your partner which may result in lack of respect for your partner. This has happened repeatedly in several homes. Try and resolve matters between yourselves, for unresolved cases you should seek counselling from your pastor or mentor.

Nabal and Abigail I Samuel 25:2-31

It's a long read, therefore I will summarize and quote the main verses.

Nabal was a very rich man. He had three thousand sheep and a thousand goats.

Abigail, his wife was a woman of good understanding and beautiful in appearance but the man was harsh and evil in his doings. Nabal was shearing his sheep which was usually a time of lavish hospitality. David heard in the wilderness that Nabal was shearing his sheep, he sent ten of his men to Nabal and to speak of how his shepherds were with them in the wilderness, his men did not hurt the shepherds rather they protected them and there was nothing missing from them while they were in the wilderness. David requested that they should be given whatever comes to Nabal's hand. When his men got to Nabal and relayed the message, Nabal's response was mean verse 11 *"Shall I then take my bread and my water and my meat that I have killed for my shearers and give it to men when I do not know where they are from?"*

David's men returned and told him all the words of Nabal. David got furious and took about four hundred men with him to descend upon Nabal, but one of Nabal's young men informed Abigail about Nabal's response to David's men. See verse 17 *"Now therefore, know and consider what you will do, for harm is determined against our master and against his entire household. <u>For he is such a scoundrel that one cannot speak to him.</u>"* Abigail made haste and took two hundred loaves of bread, two skins of wine, five sheep already dressed, five seahs of roasted grain, one hundred clusters or raisins and two hundred cakes of figs and loaded them on donkeys. When she saw David she spoke wisely and kindly to him see verse 25 *"Please, let not my lord regard this scoundrel Nabal. For as his name is, so is he: Nabal is his name, and folly is with him! But I, your maidservant, did not see the young men of my lord whom you sent."* Her words and actions moved David to revoke his decision and not only that; he fell in love with her. Nabal died ten days later, David sent and proposed to Abigail to take her as his wife.

I believe we can learn from these couples, both from their mistakes and good character. Nabal was proud, insensitive, uncaring and self-centred. He believed he knew it all and would never value what others have to offer. His servant referred to him as a scoundrel that one cannot speak to him including his wife. Nabal had a very formal relationship with his wife, he never discussed anything with her, his wife didn't know about the protection his servants received from David's men in the wilderness. The wife wasn't even aware of the visitation from David. Some women don't know the type of job their husbands do, how much they earns or their future plans because they don't communicate. I'm sure if he had communicated with wife about the protection from David's men, the wife would have advised him to find a way to reward David and his men.

If the wife knew about the visit, she would have advised him to honour them. Consider the mistakes many men have made because they refuse to involve their wives in decision making. Consider the wisdom in Abigail, David saw a treasure in her and he would not let go of it. Don't wait until you lose her before you start valuing her. Seek advice from one another before making decisions and carry yourselves along.

We are skilled in diverse areas; some men are good at fixing machinery at home. My daughter usually says *"My daddy can fix anything."* But some men are not skilled at fixing machinery but they are very good at doing other things like sports. Similarly, some men do not relate well with their wives not because they are evil, they genuinely do not know how to treat women kindly, lovingly and romantically. In such situation, it is advisable to seek knowledge – read books, attend marriage seminars, listen to inspirational messages on marriage, seek advice from your pastor or mentor.

How do we maintain effective and consistent communication with our spouses? Considering our busy and competitive environment, the husband works during the day, the wife does night shift, and there is hardly any time to spend together. First of all, you must delight in the company of one another, discuss with your partner to find a suitable time for yourselves.

If possible, find another job that would enable you both to spend time together. After all, what is the point of becoming rich at the expense of your family/marriage? I encourage couples to find time to communicate on a daily basis for a minimum of 30 minutes; this is an opportunity to discuss how your day went, burdens in your mind, future plans, compliment and encourage yourselves. Get rid of all distractions at this time namely: phones, tablets, Facebook, television, games etc. Go on dates on regular basis e.g. fortnightly. You could also arrange a family day once a week; mine is Sunday after church service.

Abraham and Sarah Genesis 16:1-6, Genesis 21:8-14, Genesis 22:1-3

In the first text Genesis 16:1-6, Abraham and Sarah had been waiting on God for the fruit of the womb. At this point Sarah was getting frustrated and unable to bear the sorrow of barrenness. She said to Abraham (then Abram) to have children by Hagar. Surprisingly, Abraham heeded the voice of Sarah. In the earlier chapter Abraham had an encounter with God and God reminded him of His promises. I'm not sure if Abraham told Sarah of this encounter (the bible didn't tell us he did) to encourage her faith. Sometimes couples operate at different levels of faith; it is important we stir up our faith and carry ourselves along in our walk with God. Yes we need to make decisions together and take input from one another. However, it is important to weigh every thought and suggestions in the spirit whether it is in accordance to the will of God. Clearly, Sarah's suggestion was not led by the Spirit. It is imperative to seek the will of God in every joint decision we make as couples.

The second text, Sarah was speaking by the spirit when she told Abraham to "*cast out this bondwoman and her son; for the son of this bondwoman shall not be heir with my son, namely with Isaac*" Genesis 21:10. Abraham didn't feel good about his wife's suggestion but this time he heard the voice of God telling him to listen to his wife and he obeyed.

The last text, God asked Abraham to sacrifice the son they had waited for, for several years. The bible didn't tell us that he told his wife. I'm sure you can imagine what Sarah's response would be if he had told her that God had asked him to sacrifice their only son. He didn't tell her because he knew his wife so well. Know yourselves well enough. Marriage is a relationship between 3 people: God, you and your spouse.

Reigniting your marriage

CHAPTER 4

God's Blueprint for Marriage

Genesis 26:24-25 "*[24] And the Lord appeared to him the same night and said, "I am the God of your father Abraham; do not fear, for I am with you, I will bless you and multiply your descendants for My servant Abraham's sake." [25] So he build an altar there and called on the name of the Lord, and he pitched his tent there; and there Isaac's servants dug a well."*

Every idea has an origin, every tree has a root, every stream has a source and every product has a creator. Mankind and marriage originated from God the Father. The Greek word for the word 'Father' is Pater which means progenitor or originator meaning he who imparts life. Marriage is God's idea and God clearly designed a pattern for marriage.

In Genesis 26:25 we were told that after God appeared to Jacob, He did 3 things:

1) He built an altar there and called upon the name of the Lord. Altar is a place of sacrifice or worship which speaks of relationship with God.

2) He pitched his tent there. In other words he built a house or more precisely a home

3) His servants dug a well. That signifies industry, business, career or ministry.

The ideal code is 123 – God, family and business. But many follow the code – 321, some do 312, some do 132, which one are you following? Of course, I am not saying you should raise a family before pursuing your career. Obviously, you need finance to enable you to raise a family. He who does not provide for his family is worse than an unbeliever - I Timothy 5:8.

Ensure you have a stable source of income before you walk down the aisle with a damsel. Money enhances 'honey' in marriage. The code is applicable in marriage where you don't attach importance to your business more than your spouse and God comes first in everything you do.

See Ecclesiastes 9:8-10 "[8.] *Let your garments always be white, and let your head lack no oil.* [9.] *Live joyfully with the wife whom you love all the days of your vain life which He has given you under the sun, all your days of vanity; for that is your portion in life, and in the labour which you perform under the sun. [10.] Whatever your hand finds to do, do it with your might; for there is no work of device or knowledge or wisdom in the grave where you are going."*

Again Solomon in the above scripture further buttresses the code 123. Verse 8 speaks of your relationship with God, verse 9 speaks of your marriage and verse 10 speaks of your business, career, ministry etc.

Your garment must always be white. White garment signifies purity. Revelation 3:4 *"You have a few names even in Sardi who have not defiled their garments."* (American King James Version). Defilement usually caused by sin separates us from God (not separate God from us). Isaiah 59:1

Reigniting your marriage

"Surely the arm of the Lord is not too short to save nor his ear too dull to hear. But your iniquities have <u>separated you from your God</u>; your sins have hidden his face from you so that He will not hear."

Living a sinful lifestyle disconnects us from God which makes it difficult to discern the will of God in any given circumstances. Unrepented sin hardens the heart and breeds rebellion against God or the things of God. If you desire to restore love and bring intimacy back into your marriage, if you desire to save your marriage, it must begin with your personal relationship with God. The fear of God is the beginning of wisdom; the wisdom to save and to keep your marriage.

Hebrews 13:4 *"Marriage is honourable among all and the bed undefiled; but*

75 | P a g e

fornicators and adulterers God will judge."
It is the fear of God that keeps you from
adultery. What keeps you faithful in your
marriage is not just your commitment to
your wife but first of all your commitment
to God.

Ephesians 5:25-27 "[25.] *Husbands love your
wives just as Christ also loved the church
and gave Himself for her,* [26.] *that He might
sanctify and cleanse her with the washing
of water by the word,* [27.] *that He might
present her to Himself a glorious church not
having spot or wrinkle or any such thing but
that she should be holy and without
blemish."* We have issues in marriage
because of the presence of spots, wrinkles
and blemishes which represents character
flaws. Most of the issues we face in
marriage are works of the flesh – anger,
impatience, infidelity, stubbornness,

unforgiveness, pride, dishonesty. My husband is handsome and very kind but when he gets angry, he's like a hurricane. My wife is beautiful and very nice but when she gets moody, it could go on for days. The word of God has the power to cleanse us from every character flaws.

Let your head lack no oil: Two people from different backgrounds coming to live together is the greatest miracle next to salvation. A peaceful marriage requires understanding. The anointing is that heavenly lubricant that helps us to attempt and attain the things we cannot do ordinarily. You need the anointing of the Holy Spirit in your marriage. The anointing does two primary things:

- **He heals us** – You may have been hurt badly by your spouse and you find it hard to relate with him/her. As we worship, He releases His anointing to heal us from pains, lifts burdens and breaks yokes. Many people live in unforgiveness not because they don't want to forgive but they find it difficult to recover from the pains their partner has caused them. But you have to make up your mind to forgive your partner, not for their sake but for your own sake. *"Forgive us our sins as we forgive those who sin against us"* Luke 11:4. Unforgiveness breeds bitterness and bitterness leads to unfruitfulness 2 Kings 2:19.

Isaiah 61:1 *"The Spirit of the Lord God is upon Me, because the Lord has anointed to.....He has sent Me to heal the broken-hearted."* I pray for you; be healed of your wounds, be healed of your broken heart in the mighty name of Jesus.

- **He empowers us to do** – what we couldn't do naturally. The power of the Holy Spirit is not limited to ministry works, but for everyday living at work, in business, in the home, at school etc. He enables to us to function as husband, as wife and as parents.

Live joyfully with the wife: Proverbs 5:18-19 *"Let your fountain be blessed, and rejoice with the wife of your youth. [19.] As a loving deer and a graceful doe, let her breasts satisfy you at all times; always be enraptured with her love."* The fountain here refers to your wife. Let your wife be blessed by making her happy; by behaving to her in a loving, adorable and respectful manner. If you make your wife happy, then you will become a happy and fulfilled husband.

The happiness of your spouse is dependent on you. Decide to make him/her happy always. Rejoice with the wife of your youth means the wife since the days of your youth, do not divorce her nor despise her even in your old age. Delight in her company, express joy and pleasure in seeing her.

Whatever your hand finds to do, do it with your might: This refers to your business, career and ministry. In I Timothy 3:1-5 *"This is a faithful saying: if a man desires the position of a bishop, he desires a good work. A bishop then must be blameless, the husband of one wife......4. One who rules his own house well, having his children in submission with all reverence*

5. (for if a man does not know how to rule his own house, how will he take care of the church of God?)"

It is a requirement for church leaders to know how to rule their home well before they get appointed. Don't pursue your ministry or career at the expense of your home. Remember, Noah could not save the people but he saved his family and that was sufficient for him.

Reigniting your marriage

CHAPTER 5

The Spirit Led Couple

My pastor and spiritual father Dr. Tunde Bakare in one of his teachings on marriage defined Marriage as One man and one woman united spiritually, emotionally, physically, publicly and legally in a life time bond of loyal love. There are six key words to buttress from this definition.

The key words are described below:

1. One man and one woman: Matthew 19:4 *"He who created them from the beginning made them male and female."*

These were the very words of our Lord Jesus Christ. When God made animals, the birds and the fishes, He made multiples of them (Genesis 1:20-25) but when the time came for mankind to be created, he made one male and one female. That is because marriage is supposed to be monogamous, a union between one man and one woman. Anything outside of that is not marriage – call it something else.

2. United Spiritually: Genesis 1:27 *"So God created man in His own image; in the image of God He created him; male and female He created them."* At creation, He made us male and female. We didn't have physical bodies; we were made in God's image. God is not tall, not short, not white, not black, not English and not American. God is Spirit and He made us

in His image, we are spirits, therefore it doesn't matter the race, colour, language and town you come from, we were all made in the image of God. Marriage is spiritual meaning that it cuts across all cultural, language or racial barriers. Spiritual union is necessary before physical union as the spiritual controls the physical. When there is spiritual bonding, it becomes easier to live in agreement. You and your spouse must be united spiritually before physically, which is why you should never put the cart before the horse by allowing sexual intercourse before the spiritual joining.

3. United Emotionally: Genesis 2:18*"And the Lord God said it is not good that man should be alone; I will make him a helper comparable to him."* Adam was not

physically alone because there were animals with him but none of the animals could connect with him emotionally, therefore a helper suitable for him was needed. Sometimes we feel lonely in our emotions despite the people being around us. In John 4, a woman had been married five times, she has had five failed marriages, and currently living with the sixth man vs 18 *"for you have had five husbands and the one whom you now have is not your husband; in that you spoke truly"* They were cohabiting. Cohabiting is not the same as marriage.

Yet she still felt unfulfilled in her emotions. Jesus was speaking figuratively, that if she drank of the water He gives, she would no longer be thirsty – she had been thirsty for something those men could not satisfy. Finally, she met the seventh man – Jesus. One of the signs that you have found the right person is that you feel emotionally fulfilled and peaceful.

4. United Physically: United physically with a ring as a symbol of their covenant and consummation as a symbol of their physical union. Hebrews 13:4 "*Marriage is honourable among all and the bed undefiled; but fornicators and adulterers God will judge.*" Marriage is honourable and should be held in great esteem. No sane person would rip in two a £50 note. The national flag is a symbol or emblem of a nation. Dishonouring the national flag is to dishonour the country the flag symbolizes. To have sexual intercourse before or outside your marriage is to dishonour the marriage institution and

ultimately dishonouring God. Genesis 2:24 *"Therefore a man shall leave his father and mother and be joined to his wife and they shall become one flesh."* There must be a leaving before a cleaving. It is not possible to be fully united with your wife if you keep giving preference to your parents, siblings, other relations or friends over your wife. By being one with your wife, it means you make decisions together, you maintain absolute honesty and transparency.

5. United Publicly: The first miracle Jesus performed was at a wedding in Cana of Galilee, to fix the first institution God created. The wedding was a public event. There is no such thing as a secret marriage. There must be witnesses. Out of two or three witnesses a truth shall be

established. Marriage may be personal but not private. When someone who is not married gets pregnant, it's not a comfortable feeling especially amongst family members but if one is married, the bump is even flaunted.

6. United Legally: God is a God of order and the government is set up to establish law and order in any given state. Romans 13:1 *"Let every soul be subject to the governing authorities, for there is no authority except from God and the authorities that exist are appointed by God."* It is therefore important that the law of the land recognises your marriage.

Once this foundation is right, then you can be sure that your marriage is as God defined it. Psalm 11:3 *"If the foundations are destroyed, what can the righteous do?"* The righteous should revisit the foundation. Review your marriage based on the key words described above.

Walk in the Spirit

Amos 3:3 *"Can two walk together, unless they are agreed?"* As mentioned in chapter one, couples must both walk in the spirit for them to be in agreement.

Galatians 5:16 *"I say then, walk in the spirit and you shall not fulfil the lust of the flesh"*

Three ways to walk in the Spirit:

1. Walk in Love: Ephesians 5:1-2 *"Therefore be imitators of God as dear children. And walk in love, as Christ also has loved us and given*

Himself for us, an offering and a sacrifice to God for a sweet-smelling aroma."

A sure way to walk in the spirit is to walk in love. With love we can manifest the fruits of the Holy Spirit in our relationships.

Love is an offering and a sacrifice to the person whom we love. Marriage is a relationship between two forgivers. Love enables us to forgive the wrongs of our partners.

I Corinthians 13:4-7 *"Love suffers long and is kind; love does not envy; love does not parade itself, is not puffed up; does not behave rudely, does not seek its own, is not provoked, thinks no evil; does not rejoice in iniquity but rejoices in the truth; bears all things, believes all things, hopes all things, endures all things."*

This kind of love is not based on feelings, or looks or what we can get. It is supplied by the Holy Spirit. Romans 5:5 *"Now hope does not disappoint because the love of God has been poured out in our hearts by the Holy Spirit who was given to us"*. When you become angry with your spouse or you have a feeling of displeasure towards them, talk to the Holy Spirit and He would heal your heart, fill your heart with love and would tell you what to do.

Joseph got displeased with Mary because she was found pregnant; how would you feel if your fiancée got pregnant by another person? The natural response was to put an end to that relationship but while he was considering a secret disengagement an Angel of the Lord appeared to him and told Him what to do (Matthew 1:18-20).

If he had put her away, he would have rejected his destiny. Many damages have been done in many relationships, families and destinies as a result of uncontrolled anger.

Ephesians 4:25-27 "25 *Therefore putting away lying, let each one of you speak the truth with his neighbour, for we are members of one another,* 26 *be angry and do not sin: do not let the sun go down on your wrath* 27 *nor give place to the devil.*" When we allow anger to get hold of us, we give place to the devil in our relationships.

2. Walk in Light: Ephesians 5: 8-11 "[8] *For you were once darkness, but now you are light in the Lord. Walk as children of light [9] for the fruit of the Spirit is in all goodness, righteousness and truth [10] finding out what is acceptable to the Lord.*" The bible calls you a child of light, therefore your words and actions should reflect the light that you are. God is light and there is no darkness in Him. Darkness represents evil works while light represents the fruit of the Spirit: goodness, righteousness and truth. Whenever there is a conflict in your relationship, you must bear in mind that it is not about who is wrong or who is right

but about doing what is good, right and true. These should be the ingredients of our character. Sometimes we get provoked and feel frustrated that we feel like revenging. Each time we feel tempted to make rash decisions, we should ask ourselves – is this acceptable to the Lord?

Psalm 119:130 "*The entrance of Your words gives light; It gives understanding to the simple.*" The intensity of the light you reflect is dependent on the amount of light you gain from God's Word. The Word of God has the potency to change us and to enable us to live as children of light. The knowledge of the Word gives light and weight in the spirit; therefore we don't easily react to offence or fall for the temptations the enemy brings our way.

The knowledge of the word also gives understanding on how to respond to issues. As a husband you must learn to be tender and firm in your role as the leader in the home. Being tender should be the default position but there are times when the husband needs to be firm. Example was when Eve fell for the temptation of the devil and ate the forbidden fruit and she gave some to her husband who was with her (Genesis 3:6). Adam should have stood on the instruction God gave to him and point the wife in the right direction. Another example was when Sarai introduced Hagar to her husband Abram in order to obtain children by her. Abraham should have maintained his stand on God's word and not act in the flesh (Genesis 16:1-2).

3. Walk in Wisdom: Ephesians 5:15-18 "*15See then that you walk circumspectly, not as fools but as wise, 16 redeeming the time because the days are evil. 17 Therefore do not be unwise, but understand what the will of the Lord is. 18 And do not be drunk with wine, in which is dissipation; but be filled with the Spirit*" Wisdom is the ability to live life skilfully. To walk circumspectly is to walk purposefully, worthily and accurately. What is the purpose of your relationship? A relationship without purpose is heading nowhere. If you are in a relationship with a guy, what is the aim of that relationship?

You have to find out from him what his intensions are and not fall victim of a time waster. If you are married, you must define the purpose of your marriage in God. There must be a reason why God brought you both together. After all, God gave Eve to Adam to help him fulfil his divine assignment which was to tend the Garden of Eden. Abuse sets in when purpose is not understood. A people (family) without a vision will perish (Proverbs 29:18). It is the responsibility of the man to define a vision for the home and then raise his family to pursue the vision.

The New American Standard Bible says *"Where there is no vision, the people are unrestrained....."*

proverbs 29:18. They are unrestrained from acting in the flesh, living in adultery, bitterness, anger, hate, unforgiveness, dishonesty etc.

To live purposefully is to walk in wisdom. Ephesians 4:1 "....*walk worthy of the calling with which you were called.*" Walk worthy of your calling and purpose in God. Walk worthy of your status as a married man or engaged to someone in a relationship. Remember, marriage is honourable. Live accurately, and not in error. Those who live in error will experience terror. Correct the error and the terror will cease.

Redeeming the time means making most of the time you spend together. Many couples live very busy lives, and the little time they spend together is wasted in unreasonable arguments. Determine between yourselves to enjoy every moment you spend together.

Understanding the will of God in your marriage would enable you to act in wisdom. The bible is God's will concerning us. Understanding the scriptures enables us to understand how God would act in any given situation. 'What would Jesus Do?' can be found on the pages of the scriptures.

Lastly, do not be drunk with wine, in other words do not be influenced with wine. Some people are influenced by their friends, relatives, past mistakes, circumstances; therefore they act in a manner that is displeasing to their spouses.

Instead be filled with the Spirit of God, (verse 19) speaking to your spouse in psalms and hymns and spiritual songs, encouraging words, words that edify rather than words that hurt and cause pain, appreciation, (verse 21) submitting to one another in the fear of God.

Reigniting your marriage

CHAPTER 6

Moral Code of Conduct in Marriage

According to Wikipedia, morality is from the latin word 'Moralitas' which means manner, character or appropriate behaviour. It is the differentiation of intensions, decisions and actions between those that are good or right and those that are bad or wrong.

Another word that is close to morality is Amorality which is indifference towards a set of principles or unawareness or disbelief in such principles. For example, babies are amoral in that they don't sympathize nor empathize. They cry whenever they want to, they don't care if it's appropriate for the environment or not. Adults can't claim to be amoral because we have the knowledge of good and evil. Ethics can be used interchangeably, however while morals could be personal, ethics are principles that guard a particular tradition, group of professionals.

Every professional organisation has a code of conduct which directs the behaviour of its members in professional matters. For example one of the code of conduct of the British Computer Society is that its members must not claim any level of competence that they do not possess.

If professional institutions/organisations have moral code of conduct, marriage as an institution should also have a code of conduct.

Moral code of conduct in marriage extracted from I Peter 3:1-12:

Wives, likewise, be submissive to your own husbands, that even if some do not obey the word, they, without a word, may be won by the conduct of their wives, [2] when they observe your chaste conduct accompanied by fear. [3] Do not let your adornment be merely outward— arranging the hair, wearing gold, or putting on fine apparel— [4] rather let it be the hidden person of the heart, with the incorruptible beauty of a gentle and quiet spirit, which is very precious in the sight of God. [5] For in this manner, in former times, the holy women who trusted in God also adorned themselves, being submissive to their own husbands, [6] as Sarah obeyed Abraham, calling him lord, whose daughters you are if you do good and are not afraid with any terror.

⁷Husbands, likewise, dwell with them with understanding, giving honor to the wife, as to the weaker vessel, and as being heirs together of the grace of life, that your prayers may not be hindered.

⁸Finally, all of you be of one mind, having compassion for one another; love as brothers, be tenderhearted, be courteous;[a]

⁹not returning evil for evil or reviling for reviling, but on the contrary blessing, knowing that you were called to this, that you may inherit a blessing. ¹⁰For

"He who would love life And see good days, Let him refrain his tongue from evil, And his lips from speaking deceit. ¹¹Let him turn away from evil and do good; Let him seek peace and pursue it. ¹²For the eyes of the Lord *are on the*

righteous, And His ears are open to their prayers; But the face of the LORD is against those who do evil."

1) **Submission:** I Peter 3:1*"Wives likewise be submissive to your own husbands, that even if some do not obey the word, they without a word may be won by the conduct of their wives."* To submit means to accept or yield to the authority of another. Submission is not a sign of weakness but obedience to the Lord and acceptance of your husband's authority over you. Peter didn't say submit to all men but to your own husband. The husband is the head, just as the face is used to identify a person; the husband is the face of your marriage. You agreed to become submissive to him when you changed your surname to his. You may be the MD/CEO of your company but in

your home, you must submit to your husband as your head.

2) **Respect:** Vs 2 says "*When they observe your chaste conduct accompanied by fear.*" The amplified version "*When they observe the pure and modest way in which you conduct yourselves, together with your reverence [for your husband; you are to feel for him all that reverence includes: to respect, defer to, revere him—to honour, esteem, appreciate, prize, and, in the human sense, to adore him, that is, to admire, praise, be devoted to, deeply love, and enjoy your husband*]. Men usually misinterpret love as respect; therefore as you show deep respect for your husband, you are communicating how much you love him. It is in your place to relate with your husband like a king and you will remain

the queen of his heart. Queen Vashti dishonoured her husband and she lost her place.

Be mindful of the manner in which you talk to your husband. Don't talk to him as if you are his supervisor, don't talk to him as if you are in-charge, don't talk to him as if he is your errand boy. Mind your tone when talking. Even if your husband is not as smart as you are, the Lord has put you in his life to complement him and not to compete with him. When you correct him, don't insult his intelligence.

3) **Gentle and peaceful spirit:** verse 4 *"rather let it be the hidden person of the heart, with the incorruptible beauty of a gentle and quiet spirit, which is very precious in the sight of God."* Not a feisty spirit, not a lousy spirit, not a nagging spirit, but a gentle and quiet spirit. A

gentle and quiet spirit is a product of your maturity in God. If women spend time to beautify their spirit as much the time they spend in beautifying their body, they would respond better to situations.

Seek peace and pursue it. James 3:18 *"Now the fruit of righteousness is sown in peace by those who make peace"* The evidence of your righteousness is the pursuance of peace. Be a peacemaker. Blessed are the peace makers for they shall be called the sons of God. Don't always wait for your husband to make the first move to settle issues. Make the first move; ensure peace reigns in your home.

4) **Be considerate:** verse 7 *"Husbands, likewise <u>dwell with them with understanding</u>, giving honour to the wife, as to the weaker vessel, and as being*

heirs together of the grace of life, that your prayers may not be hindered." To be understanding is to be considerate. The woman goes to work, comes back home to cook for the family, does the laundry, looks after the baby, does the house cleaning with little or no support from her husband, yet the husband doesn't show his appreciation instead complains that she's starving him of sex. Of course she's tired. A woman complained bitterly about how her husband would not help out in the home; she said she was being treated like a slave – but the husband didn't see it that way. He said *'I go to work and my wife stays at home and work. After all, they are both working.'* House chores and office work are not the same. Support your wife in house chores.

5) **Honour your wife:** "*...giving honour to the wife as to the weaker vessel*". Weaker vessel here isn't referring to weakness in strength or being inferior rather it means as one would treat a very precious possession with care. Honour your wife; appreciate her for all the support she has rendered. If you haven't celebrated your wife in a while, use the next seven days to express how much you appreciate her. What we appreciate increase in value.

6) **Defend your wife:** Part of honouring your wife is defending her and not making her a public spectacle as King Ahasuerus did. Defend her before your relatives, friends and people. Don't discuss your spouse with a third party. It is the image you portray about your spouse that determines how she is perceived.

7) **Don't accommodate strife:** Proverbs 17:9 *"He who covers a transgression seeks love, but he who repeats a matter separates friends."* Love covers multitude of sin. Love does not find fault rather it overlooks. That does not mean issues should be swept under the carpet, I believe issues should be discussed constructively with the aim of coming to an agreement. I also believe that if your spouse raises a concern, it is inappropriate to dismiss such concern as if it is of no importance. Concerns should be given appropriate attention by discussing them. Once resolved both of you should ensure you keep your side of the agreement and endeavour not to bring up such concerns again unless no or inadequate commitment is shown by your spouse to keep their side of the

bargain. Repeating settled issues destroys relationship rather than building it.

8) **Pray together:** Peter said you both are heirs of the **grace of life** that your prayers may not be hindered (verse 7). It is expected that couples should pray together. A couple that prays together stays together and you both become partakers of the grace of life. When strife exists between couples, it tends to frustrate that grace and prayers become hindered. Your prayer to God is seen as a cheque with two signatories; if you are not in agreement with your spouse, your cheque will not be honoured because the second signature is missing. Remember Jesus said "*if you bring your gift to the altar, and there remember that your brother has something against*

you, [24] *leave your gift there before the altar, and go your way. First be reconciled to your brother, and then come and offer your gift."* Matthew 5:23-24

9) **Be of the same mind:** Be united in the spirit. Spiritual union is attained via fellowshipping with one another. When you are united spiritually, you argue less and you think alike.

10) **Be compassionate and tender-hearted:** Be sympathetic, be merciful to one another. Be tolerant and don't be too hard on your spouse. A tender heart is an affectionate heart, a heart that is easily affected with love, pity or sorrow. Your home should not be a military camp.

11) **Non-revengeful**: Verse 9 "Not returning evil for evil..." Two wrongs do not make a right. Do not be overcome with evil but rather return evil with good. Your spouse may be unkind to you but don't allow the negative actions or attitude of others to change you from being the godly person that you are. Would you be a thermometer or a thermostat? A thermometer is influenced by its environment but a thermostat changes its environment. If your spouse is unkind to you, go to God in prayers and ask Him to make them the kind of husband/wife you desire. Prayer works and God is still in the business of changing hearts. The hearts of kings are in His hands and He can direct them where He pleases. May He direct the heart of your spouse to you in Jesus' precious name. Amen.

12) **Refrain your tongue from evil:** James 3:2 "*For we all stumble in many things. If anyone does not stumble in word, <u>he is a perfect man</u>, able also to bridle the whole body.*" One of the ways to enjoy a perfect marriage is not to stumble in word. Saying the wrong things can spark up argument, destroy the day and ruin a romantic dinner. You need the wisdom to choose your words and to say the right things at the right time.

Avoid making careless or provoking statements. Ensure no insults or offensive words proceed from your mouth including lies. Some homes have been polluted with negative words making it difficult for life to spring up in such environment. Decide to utter positive words. Colossians 4:6 "*Let your speech always be with grace, seasoned with salt, that you may know how you ought to answer each one.*" Let your speech be seasoned with God's word by being filled with the word.

Establishing Family Values

In addition to code of conduct, it is important we establish family values. Values and code of conduct are very similar but are slightly different. Codes of conduct are rules that are set by an organisation to guide the behaviour of her professional members while values are the principles, philosophies which help to define how an organisation functions or behaves.

There are big corporations, organisations with core values, their values serve as a compass, helping them to set and maintain the right direction for their business. Their values remain valid wherever their business takes them to. Their situations don't just determine their decisions, their values inform their decision.

Toyota has eight core values, two of the values are: Customer Satisfaction and Quality in everything they do. In 2009, Toyota recalled 3.8 million vehicles in the USA because of floor mat problems which could make the accelerator get stuck.

A few years ago they recalled almost 5,500 third generation Yaris models in the UK to fix problems with the powered steering because they have zero-tolerance approach on quality issues affecting their vehicles.
Their product had fault, they didn't ignore it. They looked for a solution. Values are reasons or justification for doing things. It is your value system that drives you.

The president of one of the most famous countries in the world comes home to have dinner with his family regardless of how busy he is. That is the value of commitment – commitment to his wife and children.

Apart from values being reasons or justifications for doing things; values help determine boundaries. Imagine you driving on the high way without road markings accidents are more likely to happen. So values are established guidelines for living.

Joseph would have sold his future for a few minutes of enjoyment if he didn't have values. Joseph didn't just make an instant decision not to sleep with Potiphar's wife, he made that decision a long time ago. How can I do this thing and sin against my God? A person without values cannot command value.

I made a decision when I was 15 years old that my first girlfriend will become my wife. Yes it did happen. Values are set principles upon which your life is built.

The fruit of the Holy Spirit are values we should live by. Have the fruits and you will be the most perfect person on earth. The values we embrace determine our response in any given circumstance. I would like to share with you the 24 values that drive my family. Write yours, print it out, share with your spouse and paste it where it can be seen every day.

Values that drive my family
1. Fellowship together
2. Do things together
3. Verbal affirmation of love, appreciation and apologise when I am wrong

4. Practical show of genuine love and concern
5. Trust
6. Protect one another (relatives and friends – don't speak evil of my partner)
7. Security (emotional, financial, future)
8. Integrity and Honesty
9. Resolve conflicts before going to sleep
10. Never raise voice during arguments
11. Never get violent
12. Never involve 3rd parties (seek counsel from my mentor/pastor if necessary)
13. Communicate timely, clearly and openly (freedom of speech)
14. Never jump into conclusions
15. Transparency (no secrets)
16. Listening (attentively)
17. Mutual respect
18. Mutual support in house chores
19. Mutual consent

20. Mutual sexual satisfaction (my aim is to please her)
21. Willingness to make sacrifices (selflessness)
22. Spend quality time together
23. Forgiveness
24. Be Spirit led

Reigniting your marriage

CHAPTER 7

Protect your Marriage

I believe by now the Holy Spirit must have revealed to you the loosed bolts and nuts in your relationship. The aim of this book is to help restore intimacy between you and your spouse by His grace alone. This last chapter will show you how to protect your marriage against separation.

Ephesians 6:13 *"Therefore take up the whole armour of God, that you may be able to withstand in the evil day and having done all, to stand."*

This chapter will enable you to withstand every opposition in your marriage and be able to stand and finish strong.

I want to describe 28 issues that can lead to divorce if not addressed; some of them have been mentioned indirectly in the previous chapters:

1. Communication problems: As oxygen is required to breathe so is communication required for the survival of any relationship. Where there is lack of communication, information is deficient, where there is deficient information, there is poor understanding of one another leading to frequent arguments, hurts and hate. When communication stops, your relationship dies. Pastor John Hagee said *"Communication is not out yelling or outtalking your partner.*

Intimidating your partner through temper isn't communication. Communication is giving your partner the freedom to disagree with you without flying into rage." Communication takes place when you and your partner can relax and talk to each other about your feelings, likes, dislikes, aspirations, issues, appreciations, regrets, desires, pains etc. Think about the following questions: Do you prefer to watch TV, play games, browse social media, stay on your phone, be with friends at the expense of your time together with your partner? Do you avoid discussing issues or would you wait for your partner to raise them? Do you prefer to withdraw when you are hurt? If your answer to any of

these questions is yes, then you need
to adjust where necessary.

2. Incompatibility: Incompatibility is
   inability to exist together in
   harmony. There are several factors
   responsible for incompatibility such
   as lifestyle, reasoning, character,
   past experiences, temperament,
   background, education, exposure
   etc. If a bird should marry a fish,
   where would they build their home?
   Marriage involves the fusion of
   individuals and families.
   Compatibility problem could be
   difference in personalities. You may
   be an introvert and your husband
   may be an extrovert, he finds it easy
   to relate with people, make friends,
   people like him including the opposite
   sex. Are you comfortable with this? I

believe compatibility issues can be resolved if there is understanding and if we allow the Holy Spirit to mould us.

3. Financial hardship: Trying times can be difficult to manage especially if the husband is unemployed or on low income. Do you both agree before you spend? What are your spending habits? Faith and patience is required during such hard times. Hebrews 6:9 "*But beloved we are confident of better things concerning you, yes the things that accompany salvation, though we speak in this manner.*" There are better things concerning your life, your marriage and your future. Hebrews 6:12 "*that you do not become sluggish (spiritually dull or loosing heart – my emphasis), but*

imitate those who through faith and patience inherit the promises." Pray together, study the word together, grow together. May the Lord perfect all that concerns you and make you overcome all hardships in Jesus' mighty name.

4. Dissatisfaction and complaints: Dissatisfaction occurs when expectations are not being met either spiritually, emotionally, financially or sexually. Again, we can understand areas of dissatisfaction when we communicate together. Listen to your spouse and try not to dismiss what they are saying.

5. Depression: There are different reasons for depression. A man left a note for his wife and he walked out of his house, he never came back and

was never found again. The note read *"I'm so tired."* It is important you look after yourselves, to make yourselves happy. The home should be a relaxation centre to deal with stress from the outside world. Make your home a stress free environment.

6. Existence of premarital children: Does it bother you that your intended spouse has premarital children? Have you both discussed and agreed on how to relate with the parent of your child? Remember Sarah wasn't comfortable around Hagar and Ishmael.

7. Delayed conception: Waiting is not always a pleasant experience whether you are waiting at the bank,

bus stop or waiting to see the doctor. Reading through the story of Jacob and Rachel, we can see the tension and rivalry between sisters. Rachel out of desperation cried,"*Give me children or else I die*" Genesis 30:1. Elkanah married another wife because Hannah was barren. I Samuel 1:2. Remember that every delayed conception in the bible had a purpose. Keep feeding your faith and keep confessing the word. See Psalms 113:9 "*He makes the barren woman abide in the house as a joyful mother of children. Praise the Lord!*"

8. Conflict with in-laws: How does your family perceive your spouse? It is your responsibility to plant the right seed in their heart about your spouse or intended spouse. Does your partner have responsibility over

his/her siblings? If yes, you need to discuss and agree on how it is done. Ideally, your nuclear family should come first before fulfilling any other extended family responsibilities. Your marital issues should not be discussed with your extended family members.

9. Lack of love: It is possible for love to wax cold. Love is like a plant. If you put it in the right environment (soil), expose it to adequate sunlight, water it regularly and nurture the ground with manure, it will grow and blossom else it dies. It becomes necessary to create an environment that is conducive for love and nurture it with care and affection. It is not enough to express love only when things are okay, what about when

things go wrong, do you withdraw your love? Love in marriage should be unconditional. Someone defined love as giving a person what they need most when they deserve it the least at a great personal cost.

10. Tiredness arising from busy schedules: We prioritize what we consider important. Even in our busy schedules, we create time to eat, sleep, take a shower and brush our teeth. I believe you can create time for your spouse if you really want to. Include your spouse in your daily plans and don't make them the last item on your agenda, then you would be 'useless' to them because you are tired.

11. Adultery: Adultery is sinful and no excuse can be justified regardless of how logical it may sound. Couples have the responsibility to protect themselves from adultery. Remember the woman who was caught in adultery, what could have led her to find solace in the arms of another man? Could it be because the man she was married to was no longer the person she used to know? It is only natural to be drawn to an environment where you feel wanted, valued and loved. Sexual starvation can lead to adultery.

12. Resentment: Before resentment sets into a marriage, there must have been several hurts. Hurts leads to silence, silence leads to disengagement, disengagement leads to blame, blame to criticism

and then to contempt or resentment which is utter lack of respect.

13. Temptation: Temptation comes in various forms and we get tempted in areas of vulnerability. Desire for fame, riches, addiction to drugs, sex, desperation, wrong company etc are various pit holes to look out for. Pray for one another. Jesus said; *"Watch and pray that you will not fall into temptation."* Matthew 26:41. Apart from praying, we must be watchful.

14. Lack of forgiveness: Ephesians 4:32 *"And be kind to one another, tender-hearted, forgiving one another even as God in Christ forgave you."*

15. Background issues: Some issues we face in marriage are traceable to

background as well as the environmental influence on us. There are some habits we picked up from our parents, for example: if your wife grew up in a family where yelling is a normal way to communicate, her yelling may be unintentional but could lead to argument between you two. Literacy is the ability to learn, unlearn and relearn. We need to learn new and improved methods of raising our family.

16. Strongholds from the past that include trauma: Tom's mother left him at the age of 5. He grew up in a harsh and hateful environment, as a result, he had issues relating with people, he gets angry easily and feels negative about life. His wife complains that at any slight argument, Tom goes into rage. Tom's

anger problem started at a very tender age. Tom's mother was a housemaid; she was diligent at her work and always minding her own business. One unfortunate morning, she got raped by her employer who was married with children. It turned out that she got pregnant, since there was nowhere to run to for help; she continued to work as a maid as that was her only means of income. She had Tom nine months later. Her employer and his wife were very mean to her but she endured until Tom turned 5 years. Due to Tom's past experience, hurt and anger have grown to become a stronghold in his life. Such stronghold was broken by the power of the Holy Spirit when he surrendered his life to Christ. Tom is now a spirit filled believer.

17. Deep emotional hurts: When people are hurting, they need affection and care. If your partner is hurting, it is your responsibility to identify the cause of the hurt and to find solution. I usually tell my wife, she is my medicine and I am her medicine. Gracious words can heal.

18. Unresolved anger: Unresolved anger is as a result of unresolved conflicts. Find out the source of those conflicts and resolve them. Speak to your pastor if necessary.

19. Pornography and masturbation: Pornography and masturbation are both sexual immorality sins. I Corinthians 6:18 *"Flee sexual immorality. Every sin that a man*

does is outside the body, but he who commits sexual immorality sins against his own body." If you have become one body with your spouse, then you are not only sinning against your body, you are also sinning against your spouse whenever you masturbate. The solution is fleeing, abstinence – get rid of all materials both hard and digital copies including websites. Feed on the word of God daily. I Peter 2:11 *"Beloved, I beg you as sojourners and pilgrims abstain from fleshly lusts which war against the soul."* If this addiction war against your soul, then you have to engage in spiritual warfare through prayers to God. Prayer kills the flesh. Romans 8:13 *"For if you live according to the flesh you will die; but if by the Spirit you put to death the deeds of the body, you will live."* You can only put to death the deeds of the body by the Spirit. This happens in the place of daily prayers.

20. Drugs and addiction: Drugs and addiction are destructive. Decide to quit right now. Surrender your life completely to Jesus, seek counselling and make yourself accountable to your mentor/pastor.

21. A refusal to deal with problems/issues: Unless you don't want to live happily with your spouse or you don't want to confront the problems in your marriage. God said *"Come and let us reason together"* Isaiah 1:18. Nobody overcomes a problem by avoiding it. You both

have to come together to reason out the problem.

22. Immaturity: Maturity comes with knowledge and experience. *"My people perish for lack of knowledge"*. Hosea 4:6. When God asked Solomon in 1 Kings 3:5-7 *"Ask! What shall I give you?"* Solomon replied *"....Now, O Lord my God, You have made Your servant king instead of my father David, but I am a little child; I do not know how to go out or come in"*. Solomon admitted that he was immature. The he asked God for an understanding heart in verse 9. Ask God to give you the wisdom and understanding to know how to relate with your spouse. Solomon was a ferocious reader because God gave him a heart to thirst for knowledge.

Become a reader; listen to anointed sermons to increase your understanding.

23. Irresponsibility or lack of commitment: To be responsible is to have an obligation to do something or towards somebody. You are responsible for the success or the failure of your marriage. I have heard someone saying that somebody talked his wife into leaving him. You cannot hold someone else responsible for the failure of your marriage. In marriage there is no plan B. Your spouse needs that commitment that you will never leave them. Divorce should not be used to threaten your partner.

24. Not praying and sharing fellowship: As mentioned earlier in chapter four, God must come first in our relationship.

25. Unrepentant heart/Unwilling to change: If you are unwilling to make amendments regarding the issues your partner has mentioned to you, then your future with your partner is not guaranteed. Isaiah 1:19 *"If you are willing and obedient you shall eat the good of the land."* It's only if you are willing and obedient that you will eat the good of your marriage. Trust in the saving grace of Christ. Titus 2:11-12 *"For the grace of God that brings salvation has appeared to all men teaching us that, denying ungodliness and worldly lusts, we should live soberly, righteously and*

godly in the present age." Grace changes us by teaching us.

26. Distant Relationship: Distant relationship especially if the husband relocates to study abroad or to seek greener pastures. If care is not taken, distractions could occur from the opposite sex. Discipline, honesty, trust and faithfulness are required to manage a distant relationship.

27. Health: Serious health challenge could pose a strain to relationships. Stay strong together and trust in the Lord for your healing. Hebrews 10:35 *"Therefore do not cast away your confidence, which has great reward"*

28. Religious beliefs: Does your partner fear God? Does your partner pay

his/her tithe? Is your partner a committed Christian or a nominal Christian or doesn't go to church? For a person to give true love, he/she must be close and committed to God.

Reigniting your marriage

Breath of Life Faith Ministries

www.bolfm.org.uk

info@bolfm.org.uk

147 | P a g e

Reigniting your marriage

www.ingramcontent.com/pod-product-compliance
Lightning Source LLC
Chambersburg PA
CBHW060801050426
42449CB00008B/1480